MW01296303

Presented to:

Never Forget The Difference You've Made

Made in the USA
Middletown, DE
20 November 2021

52989350R00062